Grannies

First published in hardback in Great Britain
by Granada Publishing in 1984
First published in Picture Lions in 1987
This edition first published in Picture Lions in 1997

1 3 5 7 9 10 8 6 4 2

ISBN: 0 00 662845-1

Picture Lions is an imprint of the Children's Division,
part of HarperCollins Publishers Ltd,
77-85 Fulham Palace Road, Hammersmith, London W6 8JB.
Text copyright © Granada Publishing 1984
Illustrations copyright © Colin Hawkins 1984
The authors/illustrators assert the moral right to be identified
as the authors/illustrators of the work.

Printed and bound in Belgium by Proost

Grannies

Colin and Jacqui Hawkins

PictureLions

An Imprint of HarperCollinsPublishers

Who's Granny's Gran?

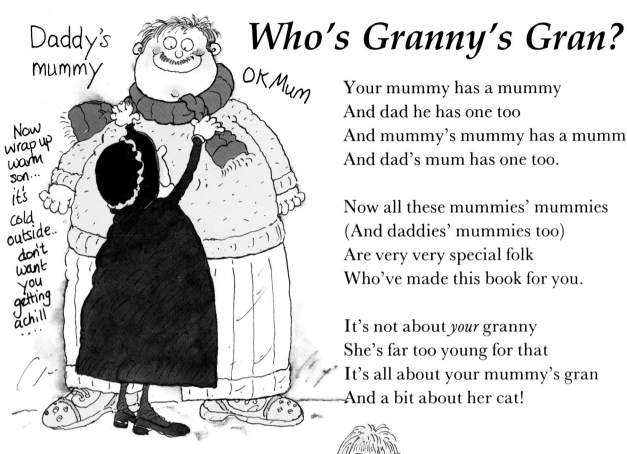

Your mummy has a mummy
And dad he has one too
And mummy's mummy has a mummy
And dad's mum has one too.

Now all these mummies' mummies
(And daddies' mummies too)
Are very very special folk
Who've made this book for you.

It's not about *your* granny
She's far too young for that
It's all about your mummy's gran
And a bit about her cat!

4

False Statements About Grannies

Often wicked tales are told
Of grannies being very old
Hard of hearing, poor of sight
With teeth that can no longer bite
Stiff old joints and snow white hair
But don't believe them
They're not fair.

Grannies can watch TV while they sleep.

Some grannies have whiskers.

Some grannies have wrinkly faces.

Why are you so wrinkly granny?

Will I have whiskers too?

Yes, dear, if you are a good girl and eat up all your cabbage.

Some grannies dye their hair.

Some grannies smell of moth balls.

Some grannies wear corsets.

What's so special about whiskers?

Some very special grannies can even take their teeth out!

Brill!

clack! clack!

Wow!

Grannies bold are more in keeping
With the stories I've been told
Always ready for an outing
Even in the bitter cold.

Granny never makes a fuss
She'll go by car, or coach or bus
(But secretly she's saving up
To buy a Honda Super Pup.)

Up the fast lane for some fun
Granny revs to do a ton
The ancient Ford goes ever faster
Even police cars cannot pass her.

She never looks to left or right
She has no mirror, has no lights
She never brakes and cannot steer
Other drivers just keep clear.

When granny rides rough,
it's awfully tough —
on her cat.

MOTORBIKE
MOLL

What about
a wheelie, gran?

Isn't it a Lovely Day

Isn't it a lovely day
When your granny comes to stay
Up the path at sprightly pace
She marches with her laden case.

She brings her cats and lots of hats
A plant for mum, a scarf for dad
Two jars of jam, a bottle of pop
A Dundee cake with nuts on top.

She kisses you, says how you've grown
She'll fatten you up, you're skin and bone
She says how much like dad you are
Not *yours* she means but your grandpa.

Then she scoops you up again
And gives you a super torch – like a pen
She says you're in for lots of treats
But just for now there's a bag of sweets.

Oh yes, and though you shouldn't really
Read such rubbish – clearly –
Here's a comic to read at night
Under the bedclothes with your new torchlight.

When Granny Comes to Stay?

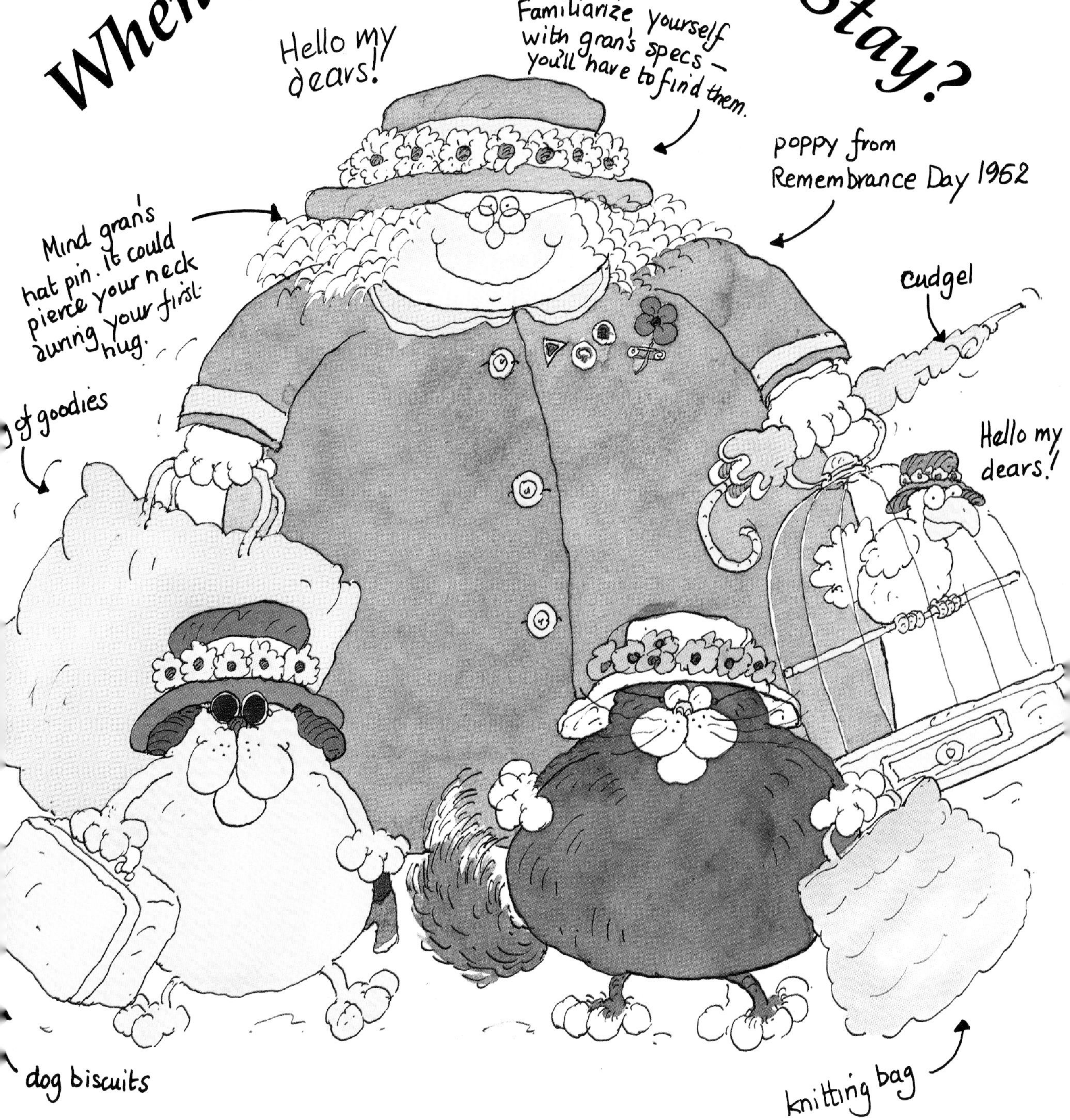

indigestion
medicine

tea cosy
no 1,468

chocs

love stories

gardening
books

letters old and new

10

nothing like a nice coal fire

creature comforts

Granny's Needs

Granny's wants are simple
Her needs are very few
A cheery room with a comfy bed
And a window with a view

A radio beside the fire
How does it work without a wire
A ticking clock with a good clear face
A few pound notes in a hiding place

A cosy chair, the Daily Mail
A box of chocs (a wee bit stale)
A decent book, a cup of tea
A nice long letter from over the sea

A TV set with screen that flickers
A drip-dry dress and bright pink knickers
A nice long chat with lots of laughs
A chance to show her photographs.

Granny's wants are simple
What she needs is you
To find her bag, her specs, her mag
And tune in to Radio 2.

Memory Lane

Gran often talks of days gone by
Of times both good and bad
She sometimes has a little cry
But not because she's sad.

She thinks about the olden days
When she was just a girl
I'll soon be gone myself, she says
But life's been quite a whirl

Gran gets on well with babies
She understands their words
She seems to know their language
(She also talks to birds!)

Little grannies sometimes have trouble getting served.

..a bottle.. ..of gin.. please

Gran keeps up her standards
She likes a little drop
Of gin or wine or fine malt Scotch
She never touches pop.

Gran doesn't like to eat too much
Perhaps a little toast
And maybe some cheese, some pie and some peas
To go with the Sunday roast.

Big grannies can ... be slow moving and wheeze a bit ... but .. they are generous to a fault with. Ice cream and second helpings.

And afterwards she'll take her pick
Jam roly-poly or spotted dick
A pink ice-cream or almond slice
A pineapple sponge would be rather nice.

I shouldn't really but I will – just this once!

It'll be indigestion pills any moment.

13

When Gran was a Girl

Things were very different
In the golden olden days
The sun was always shining
And the young had winning ways.

Girls were pretty, quiet and sweet
Boys opened doors, gave up their seat
They wore their trousers to their knees
And always said, excuse me, please.

When granny... was.. ... a .. little.. ..girl.. she had a granny of her own.

I can remember ... ... when there was only... black and white TV... ..and it was always ..fish.. on Fridays.

Granny's granny

Thank you young man

It's a pleasure

please and thankyou

Granny

Those were the days!

14

Granny.. ..thinking about the.. starving... children in China.

Of course, we wouldn't afford all the things you children have now!

In those days childen made their own.. .fun — they ..didn't.. need videos and computers.

salt... pepper

You had to finish all your food
To leave it was so very rude.
Even greens must disappear
Or else no pud or ginger beer.

But mum might give you half a penny
Quite enough for, oh, so many
Sticky buns and chocolate mice
Bars of toffee, coconut ice.

You could have some sugar plums,
A box of allsorts, a bag of gums
Some sherbet lemons and some pop
And still have change when you left the shop.

Once a month you had a bath
If you needed one or not
And every night you went to sleep
At seven on the dot.

How we.. ...loved to ..tuck our skirts in our knickers ... and skip, skip, skip...

I think I could have lasted another month

Goodnight!

Wish I had a torch!

15

16

Granny's Pets

When mummy's mummy came for the day
She brought five cats (one was a stray)
They may be lonely while I'm away
She said, if I stay for another day.

She brought her dog, her fish, her bird
They'll miss me if I stay for a third
Night, she said, and it may be a few days
More, if I stay to the end of the week.

Our dogs, they love our granny
But they're not too keen on her cats
As for the bird, they think he's absurd
And the fish, what a boring brat

It's now a month since she came for the day
All of her cats have gone astray
The fish has drowned and the bird's flown away
– least that's what our dogs say.

At the Vet's

Grannies gather at the vet's to discuss the

He's got such a big head

I'm in a bit of a flap.....

I never did like goldfish.

I wish grann wouldn't force feed me.

Couldn't resist the goldfish, dear
Now he's feeling rather queer.

I expect it's just a question
Of a little indigestion.

My Bootsy chased our neighbours' cat
Couldn't catch her, far too fat.

What did next door say to that?
Not a lot, dear, not a lot.

My dog's in a real bad temper
Got a slight touch of distemper.

Mine's got worms or could be fleas
Keep away from my Mog, please.

You ought to put that Tom away
My Mog's expecting any day.

My Tom would never soil his paws
With a mangy Mog like yours.

Granny's Guilt

When gran is here
Things disappear
And I get into trouble.

My catapult was in the drawer
Behind the kitchen door
I can't explain the window pane
It wasn't me, for sure.

I didn't drink the beastly gin
While gran was having a nap
Or fill it from the water tap
The bottle was in *her* lap.

I didn't take the piece of cake
You left for daddy's tea
It had already disappeared
With the slice for me.

Just get rid of the crumbs

Nobody would believe it!

I didn't touch the jelly, mum
I was watching telly, mum
And I didn't give the bubble gum
To the dog, mum, honest.

Nobody will miss it, just a little taste ....

ssh!

I know, dear
But never mind
Your gran comes
Only once a year.

...good heavens!

...Very funny, I don't think!

Granny is so very wise
She's rather deaf
She's got dim eyes
But she's the best one to advise
What's happening in the skies.
From low back pain
She forecasts rain
A touch of 'flu
Means snow is due
A sleeping dog
And it could be fog
She's down in the mouth
If the wind's in the south
A wheeze in her chest
And the wind's in the west
When her bones feel old
It's wintry cold
But when it's sunny
She never feels funny.

Ne'er cast a clout
'Til May be out
Is a wise old saw
But when it's hot
In March it's not –
Gran's cat thinks
It's a bore.

Granny's Wisdom

An onion hung about your neck
Will cure a nasty cold
Your eyes'll smart but it'll depart
Before one week is old.

A steak on a wart
Will make its time short

And a slap given quick
Will cure a bad hic.

Animal Wisdom

Coat your cat on the paws
With a butter pat
She'll stay home and never roam
She'll also get quite fat.

Don't put all your eggs
In one basket
Don't put any eggs
In the dog basket.

There's no point in bawling
When the milk's upset
Just lap it up, there's a pet
Or the floor will be all wet.

A bird in the hand is worth
Two in the bush
A bird in the pot is worth
Two that are not.

Granny's Garden

The plants in granny's garden
Could have no better homes
They're watered, tended – and nightly defended
By ranks of plastic gnomes.

Gran chats to every flower in turn
She grew them all from seeds
She loves them all, the small, the tall
She even loves the weeds.

Fruit and vegetables vie for space
Cabbages fight with peas
Roses ramble, brambles scramble
And beans twine round the trees.

The lawn is granny's problem
Each year worse than last
Her old push mower goes ever slower
And the grass grows twice as fast.

Squabbling starlings know that they
Can eat what fruit they win
But not, of course, blackthorn, the source
Of sloes for granny's gin.

Granny Games

My granny loves to play at games
I'm sure she likes snap best
She has great fun; she may win one
But I bet I win the rest.

Poor granny's sight is not too good
Is that a king or jack?
Is that a four? Or is it more?
Oops, snap! I've won the pack.

At draughts we are a better match
It's not the game I'd choose
My every plan seems known to gran
And in the end I lose.

I must confess I've been a cheat
Just once when granny dozed
I pinched her king so I could win
I hope her eyes were closed.

A nice sing-song round the piano.

A nice game of whist.

A nice game of charades.

Granny Makes it Better

Normally if I fall
I get up straight away
But when my granny comes to stay
I never feel so brave
I cry a bit and look so sad
She kisses me and says it's bad.
I'd better stay at home today
I needn't go to school.

Normally I go to school
I never get up late
But if granny's here I do not stir
At least 'til half past eight.
I eat a bit, but look so sick
She kisses me and says I'll lick
The bug in time. But for today
I'd better stay – in bed.

Granny's Stories

Granny tells most gripping tales
Of highwaymen and great white whales
Of ghosts and ghouls and green-faced witches
My sister is scared, but I'm in stitches.

Goodbye Granny

It's sad for us to see you board
The greenline bus for home.
You hug us and you shed a tear
'I'll be back for Christmas dear.'

Oh dear granny, we love you so
It's such a shame you have to go

Come back soon!